1,000,000 Books

are available to read at

www.ForgottenBooks.com

Read online
Download PDF
Purchase in print

ISBN 978-1-334-98964-3
PIBN 10783854

This book is a reproduction of an important historical work. Forgotten Books uses state-of-the-art technology to digitally reconstruct the work, preserving the original format whilst repairing imperfections present in the aged copy. In rare cases, an imperfection in the original, such as a blemish or missing page, may be replicated in our edition. We do, however, repair the vast majority of imperfections successfully; any imperfections that remain are intentionally left to preserve the state of such historical works.

Forgotten Books is a registered trademark of FB &c Ltd.
Copyright © 2018 FB &c Ltd.
FB &c Ltd, Dalton House, 60 Windsor Avenue, London, SW19 2RR.
Company number 08720141. Registered in England and Wales.

For support please visit www.forgottenbooks.com

1 MONTH OF FREE READING

at

www.ForgottenBooks.com

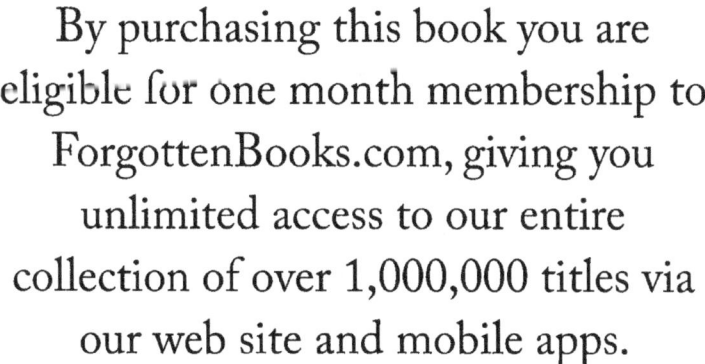

By purchasing this book you are eligible for one month membership to ForgottenBooks.com, giving you unlimited access to our entire collection of over 1,000,000 titles via our web site and mobile apps.

To claim your free month visit: www.forgottenbooks.com/free783854

* Offer is valid for 45 days from date of purchase. Terms and conditions apply.

English
Français
Deutsche
Italiano
Español
Português

www.forgottenbooks.com

Mythology Photography **Fiction**
Fishing Christianity **Art** Cooking
Essays Buddhism Freemasonry
Medicine **Biology** Music **Ancient Egypt** Evolution Carpentry Physics
Dance Geology **Mathematics** Fitness
Shakespeare **Folklore** Yoga Marketing
Confidence Immortality Biographies
Poetry **Psychology** Witchcraft
Electronics Chemistry History **Law**
Accounting **Philosophy** Anthropology
Alchemy Drama Quantum Mechanics
Atheism Sexual Health **Ancient History**
Entrepreneurship Languages Sport
Paleontology Needlework Islam
Metaphysics Investment Archaeology
Parenting Statistics Criminology
Motivational

Harvard Law School

is Rawle

...nal Law and Arbitration.

HE ANNUAL ADDRESS

DELIVERED BEFORE THE

...AN BAR ASSOCIATION,

AT

...ings, Thursday, August 20, 1896,

BY

...L OF KILLOWEN, G. C. M. G., LL.D.

...RD CHIEF JUSTICE OF ENGLAND.)

...om the Transactions of the Association.]

HARVARD LAW LIBRARY

Received Oct. 26, 1896

International Law and Arbitration.

THE ANNUAL ADDRESS

DELIVERED BEFORE THE

AMERICAN BAR ASSOCIATION,

AT

Saratoga Springs, Thursday, August 20, 1896,

BY

LORD RUSSELL OF KILLOWEN, G. C. M. G., LL.D.

(LORD CHIEF JUSTICE OF ENGLAND.)

[Reprinted from the Transactions of the Association.]

Rec. Oct. 26, 1896

INTERNATIONAL LAW

AND

ARBITRATION.

Mr. President:

My first words must be in acknowledgment of the honor done me, by inviting me to address you on this interesting occasion. You are a Congress of Lawyers of the United States met together to take counsel, in no narrow spirit, on questions affecting the interests of your Profession; to consider necessary amendments in the Law which experience and time develop; and to examine the current of judicial decision and of legislation, State and Federal, and whither that current tends. I, on the other hand, come from the judicial Bench of a distant land, and yet I do not feel that I am a stranger amongst you, nor do you, I think, regard me as a stranger. Though we represent political communities which differ widely in many respects, in the structure of their constitutions and otherwise, we yet have many things in common.

We speak the same language; we administer Laws based on the same juridical conceptions; we are co-heirs in the rich traditions of political freedom long established, and, we enjoy in common a literature, the noblest and the purest the world has known—an accumulated store of centuries to which you, on your part, have made generous contribution. Beyond this, the unseen "crimson thread" of kinship, stretching from the mother Islands to your great Continent, unites us, and reminds us always that we belong to the same, though a mixed, racial family. Indeed the spectacle which we, to-day, present is unique. We represent the great English-speaking communities—communities occupying a large space of the surface of the Earth—made up of races wherein the blood of Celt and Saxon, of Dane and Norman, of Pict and Scot, are mingled and fused into an aggregate power held together by the nexus of a common speech—combining at once territorial dominion, political influence and intellectual force greater than History records in the case of any other people.

This consideration is prominent amongst those which suggest the theme on which I desire to address you—namely, International Law.

The English-speaking peoples, masters not alone of extended territory but also of a mighty commerce, the energy and enterprise of whose sons have made them the great Travellers and Colonizers of the world—have interests to safeguard in every quarter of it, and, therefore, in an especial manner it is important to them, that the Rules which govern the relations of States *inter se* should be well understood and should rest on the solid bases of convenience, of justice and of reason. One other consideration has prompted the selection of my subject. I knew it was one which could not fail, however imperfectly treated, to interest you. You regard with just pride the part which the Judges and writers of the United States have played in the development of International Law. Story, Kent, Marshall, Wheaton, Dana, Woolsey, Halleck and Wharton, amongst others, compare not unfavorably with the workers of any age, in this province of jurisprudence.

International Law, then, is my subject. The necessities of my position restrict me to, at best, a cursory and perfunctory treatment of it.

I propose briefly to consider what is International Law; its sources; the standard—the ethical standard—to which it ought to conform; the characteristics of its modern tendencies and developments, and then to add some (I think) needful words on the question, lately so much discussed, of International Arbitration.

I call the Rules which civilized nations have agreed shall bind them in their conduct *inter se*, by the Benthamite title, "International Law." And here, Mr. President, on the threshold of my subject I find an obstacle in my way. My right so to describe them is challenged. It is said by some that there is no International Law, that there is only a bundle, more or less confused, of rules to which nations more or less conform, but that International Law there is none. The late Sir James F. Stephen takes this view in his History of the Criminal Law of England, and in the celebrated "Franconia" case (to which I shall hereafter have occasion to allude) the late Lord Coleridge speaks in the same sense. He says: "Strictly speaking, 'International Law' is an inexact expression and it is apt to mislead if its inexactness is not kept in mind. Law implies a Lawgiver and a Tribunal capable of enforcing it and coercing its transgressors." Indeed it may be said that with few exceptions the same note is sounded throughout the judgments in that case. These views, it will at once be seen, are based on the definition of Law by Austin in his "Province of Jurisprudence determined," namely, that a Law is the command of a superior who has coercive power to compel obedience and punish disobedience. But this definition is too narrow; it relies too much on force as the governing idea. If the development of Law is historically considered, it will be found to exclude that body of customary law which in early stages of Society precedes Law which assumes, definitely, the character of positive command coupled with punitive sanctions. But even in Societies in which the machinery exists for the making of Law in the Austinian sense, rules or customs grow up which are laws in every real sense of the word, as for example, the Law Merchant. Under later developments of arbitrary power Laws may be regarded as the command of a Superior with a coercive power in Austin's sense: *Quod placuit principi legis vigorem habet*. In stages later still, as government becomes more frankly democratic, resting broadly on the popular will, Laws bear less and less the character of commands imposed by a coercive authority, and acquire more and more the character of customary law founded on consent. Savigny, indeed, says of all law, that it is first developed by usage and popular faith, then by Legislation and always by internal silently-operating powers, and not mainly by the arbitrary will of the Lawgiver.

I claim, then, that the aggregate of the Rules to which nations have agreed to conform in their conduct towards one another are properly to be designated "International Law."

The celebrated author of "Ecclesiastical Polity," the "judicious" Hooker, speaking of the Austinians of his time, says: "They who are thus accustomed to speak apply the name of Law unto that only rule of working which superior authority imposeth, whereas we, somewhat more enlarging the sense thereof, term every kind of rule or canon whereby actions are framed a Law." I think it cannot be doubted that this is nearer to the true and scientific meaning of Law.

What, then, is International Law?

I know no better definition of it than that it is the sum of the Rules or Usages which civilized states have agreed shall be binding upon them in their dealings with one another.

Is this accurate and exhaustive? Is there any *a priori* rule of right or of reason or of morality which, apart from and independent of the consent of nations, is part of the Law of Nations? Is there a Law which Nature teaches, and which, by its own force, forms a component part of the Law of Nations? Was Grotius wrong when to International Law he applied the test "*placuit-ne Gentibus*"?

These were points somewhat in controversy between my learned friends, Mr. Phelps and Mr. Carter, and myself before the Paris Tribunal of Arbitration in 1893, and I have recently received from Mr. Carter a friendly invitation again to approach them—this time in a judicial rather than in a forensic spirit. I have reconsidered the matter, and, after the best consideration which I can give to the subject, I stand by the proposition which in 1893 I sought to establish. That proposition was that International Law was neither more nor less than what civilized nations have agreed shall be binding on one another as International Law.

Appeals are made to the Law of Nature and the Law of Morals, sometimes as if they were the same things, sometimes as if they were different things, sometimes as if they were in themselves International Law, and sometimes as if they enshrined immutable principles which were to be deemed to be not only part of International Law, but, if I may so say, to have been pre-ordained. I do not stop to point out in detail how many different meanings have been given to these phrases —the Law of Nature and the Law of Morals. Hardly any two writers speak of them in the same sense. No doubt appeals to both are to be found scattered loosely here and there in the opinions of Continental writers.

Let us examine them.

What is the Law of Nature?

Moralists tell us that for the individual man life is a struggle to overcome nature, and in early and, what we call natural or barbarous states of Society, the arbitrary rule of force and not of Abstract Right or Justice is the first to assert itself. In truth, the initial difficulty is to fix what is meant by the Law of Nature. Gaius speaks of it as being the same thing as the *Jus Gentium* of the Romans, which, I need not remind you, is not the same thing as *Jus inter Gentes*. Ulpian speaks of the *Jus naturale* as that in which men and animals agree. Grotius uses the term as equivalent to the *Jus stricte dictum*, to be completed in the action of a good man or state by a higher morality, but suggesting the standard to which Law ought to conform. Pufendorf in effect treats his view of the rules of abstract propriety, resting merely on unauthorized speculations, as constituting International Law and acquiring no additional authority from the usage of nations; so that he cuts off much of what Grotius regards as Law. Ortolan, in his "Diplomatie de la Mer," cites with approval the following incisive passage from Bentham, speaking of so-called natural rights springing from so-called natural law:—

"Natural right is often employed in a sense opposed to Law, as when it is said, for example, that Law cannot be opposed to Natural right, the word 'right' is employed in a sense superior to Law, a right is recognized which attacks laws, upsets and annuls it. In this sense, which is antagonistic to law, the word 'droit' is the greatest enemy of reason and the most terrible destroyer of governments.

"We cannot reason with fanatics armed with a natural right, which each one understands as he pleases, applies as it suits him, of which he will yield nothing, withdraw nothing, which is inflexible, at the same time that it is unintelligible, which is consecrated in his eyes like a dogma and which he cannot discard without a cry. Instead of examining laws by their results, instead of judging them to be good or bad, they consider them with regard to their relation to this so-called natural right. That is to say, they substitute for the reason of experience all the chimeras of their own imagination."

Austin, also, in his work on Jurisprudence, already mentioned, and referring to Pufendorf and others of his school, says:—

"They have confounded positive international morality or the rules which actually obtain amongst civilized nations in their mutual intercourse, with their own vague conceptions of international morality as it ought to be, with that indeterminate something which they call the law of nature. Professor von Martens of Gottingen is actually the first of the writers on the law of nations, who has seized this distinction with a firm grasp; the first who has distinguished the rules which ought to be received in the intercourse of nations, or, which would be received if they conformed to an assumed standard of whatever kind, from those which *are* so received, endeavored to collect from the practice of civilized communities what are the rules actually recognized and acted upon by them and gave to these rules the name of positive international law."

Finally Woolsey, speaking of this class of writers, says they commit the fault of failing to distinguish sufficiently between natural justice and the law of nations, of spinning the web of a system out of their own brain as if they were the Legislators of the world, and of neglecting to inform us what the World actually holds the Law to be by which nations regulate their conduct. So much for the law of Nature.

What are we to say of the appeal to the Law of Morality?

It cannot be affirmed that there is a universally accepted standard of morality. Then what is to be the standard? The standard of what nation? The standard of what nation and in what age?

Human society is progressive—progressive let us hope to a higher, a purer, a more unselfish ethical standard. The Mosaic Law enjoined the principle of an eye for an eye, a tooth for a tooth. The Christian law enjoins that we love our enemies and that we do good to those who hate us. But more. Nations although progressing, let us believe, in the sense which I have indicated, do not progress *pari passu*. One instance occurs to me pertinent to the subject in hand.

Take the case of Privateering. The United States is to-day the only great power which has not given its adhesion to the principle of the Declaration of Paris of 1856, for the abolition of Privateering. The other great nations of the earth have denounced Privateering as immoral and as the cover and the fruitful occasion of Piracy. I am not at all concerned to discuss in this connection whether the United States were right or were wrong. It would not be pertinent to the point; but it is just to add that the assenting Powers had not scrupled to resort to Privateering in past times, and also that the United States declared their willingness to abandon the practice if more complete immunity of private property in time of war were secured.

Nor do Nations, even where they are agreed on the inhumanity and immorality of given practices, straightway proceed to condemn them as international crimes. Take as an example of this the Slave Trade. It is not too much to say that the civilized Powers are abreast of one another in condemnation of the traffic in human beings as an unclean thing—abhorent to all principles of humanity and morality, and yet they have not yet agreed to declare this offence against humanity and morality to be an offence against the Law of Nations. That it is not so has been affirmed by English and by American Judges alike. Speaking of morality in connection with International Law, Professor Westlake in his "Principles of International Law" acutely observes that while the rules by which nations have agreed to regulate their conduct *inter se*, are alone properly to be considered International Law, these do not necessarily exhaust the ethical duties of States one to another, any more, indeed, than municipal law exhausts the ethical duties of man to man; and Dr. Whewell has remarked of jural laws in general that they are not (and perhaps it is not desirable that they should be) co-extensive with morality. He says the adjective *right* belongs to the domain of morality; the substantive *right* to the domain of law.

The truth is that civilized men have at all times been apt to recognize the existence of a Law of Morality, more or less vague and undefined, depending upon no human authority and supported by no human external sanction other than the approval and disapproval of their fellow men, yet determining, largely, for all men and societies of men what is right and wrong in human conduct, and binding, as is sometimes said, *in foro conscientiæ*. This Law of Morality is sometimes treated as syonymous with the Natural Law, but sometimes the Natural Law is regarded as having a wider sphere, including the whole Law of Morality. It cannot be said either of International Law or of Municipal Law that they include the Moral Law nor accurately or strictly that they are included within it. It is a truism to say that Municipal Law and International Law ought not to offend against the Law of Morality. They may adopt and incorporate particular precepts of the Law of Morality; and on the other hand, undoubtedly, that may be forbidden by the Municipal or International Law, which in itself is in no way contrary to the Law of Morality or of Nature. But whilst the conception of the Moral Law or Law of Nature excludes all idea of dependence on human authority, it is of the essence of Municipal Law that its rules have been either enacted or in some way recognised as binding by the supreme authority of the State (whatever that authority may be), and so also is it of the essence of International Law that its rules have been recognised as binding by the Nations constituting the community of civilized mankind.

We conclude then that, while the aim ought to be to raise high its ethical standard, International Law, as such, includes only so much of the Law of Morals or of right reason or of natural law (whatever these phrases may cover) as nations have agreed to regard as International Law.

In fine, International Law is but the sum of those rules which civilized mankind have agreed to hold as binding in the mutual relations of States. We do not indeed find all those rules recorded in clear language—there is no International code. We look for them in the long records of customary action; in settled precedents; in Treaties affirming principles; in state documents; in declarations of nations in conclave— which draw to themselves the adhesion of other nations; in declarations of Text writers of authority generally accepted, and lastly, and with most precision, in the field which they cover, in the authoritative decisions of Prize Courts. I need hardly stop to point out the great work under the last head accomplished, amongst others, by Marshall and Story in these States, by Lord Stowell in England and by Portalis in France.

From these sources we get the evidence which determines whether or not a particular canon of conduct, or a particular principle, has or has not received the express or implied assent of nations. But International Law is not as the twelve Tables of ancient Rome. It is not a closed book. Mankind are not stationary. Gradual change and gradual growth of opinion are silently going on. Opinions, doctrines, usages, advocated by acute thinkers are making their way in the world of thought. They are not yet part of the Law of Nations. In truth, neither doctrines derived from what is called the Law of Nature (in any of its various meanings) nor philanthropic ideas, however just or humane, nor the opinions of Text writers, however eminent, nor the usages of individual states—none of these, nor all combined, constitute International Law.

If we depart from the solid ground I have indicated, we find ourselves amid the treacherous quicksands of metaphysical and ethical speculation; we are bewildered, particularly by the French writers in their love for *un systeme*, and perplexed by the obscure subtleties of writers like Hautefeuille with his *Loi primitive* and *Loi secondaire*. Indeed it may, in passing, be remarked that History records no case of a controversy between nations having been settled by abstract appeals to the Laws of Nature or of Morals.

But while maintaining this position, I agree with Woolsey when he says that if International Law were not made up of rules for which reasons could be given, satisfactory to man's intellectual and moral nature, it would not deserve the name of a Science. Happily those reasons can be given. Happily men and nations propose to themselves higher and still higher ethical standards. The ultimate aim in the actions of men and of communities ought, and I presume will be admitted, to be, to conform to the divine precept, "Do unto others as you would that others should do unto you."

I have said that the rules of International Law are not to be traced with the comparative distinctness with which Municipal Law may be ascertained—although even this is not always easy. I would not have it, however, understood that I should to-day advocate the codification of International Law. The attempt has been made, as you know, by Field in this country and by Professor Bluntschli, of Heidelberg, and by some Italian jurists, but has made little way towards success. Indeed, Codification has a tendency to arrest progress. It has been so found, even where branches or heads of Municipal Law have been codified, and it will at once be seen how much less favourable a field for such an enterprise International Law presents, where so many questions are still indeterminate. After all it is to be remembered that jural law in its widest sense, is as old as Society itself; *ubi societas ibi jus est*; but International Law, as we know it, is a modern invention. It is in a state of growth and transition. To codify it would be to crystallize it; uncodified it is more flexible and more easily assimilates new rules. While agreeing, therefore, that indeterminate points should be determined and that we should aim at raising the ethical standard, I do not think we have yet reached the point at which codification is practicable or if practicable would be a public good.

Let me give give you an analogy. Amongst the most successful experiments in codification, in English communities, have been those in Anglo-India, particularly the Penal Code and the Codes of Criminal and Civil Procedure. Prompted by their comparative success, Sir Roland Wilson urged the extension of the process of codification to those traditional unwritten native usages, or customary law, of Hindu or Mahomedan origin, still recognized in the government of India by Englishmen. But the wiser opinion of Indian experts was, that it was better not to persevere in the attempt. Many of these usages, by sheer force of contact with European life and habits of thought are falling into desuetude. The hand of change is at work upon them, and to codify them would be to stop the natural progress of disintegration.

As we are not to-day considering the history of International Law, I shall say but a word as to its rise and then pass on to the consideration of its later developments and tendencies.

Like all Law, in the history of human societies, it begins with usage and custom, and unlike Municipal Law, it ends there. When, after the break-up of the Roman Empire the surface of Europe was partitioned and fell under the Rule of different sovereigns, the need was speedily felt for some guiding rule of International conduct. International Law was in a rudimentary stage; it spoke with ambiguous voice, it failed to cover the whole ground of doubtful action. It needed not only an Interpreter of authority but one who should play at once the part of mediator, arbiter and Judge. The Christian religion has done much to soften and humanize the action of men and of nations and the Papal Head of Christendom became, after the disruption of the Roman Empire, the Interpreter and almost the embodiment of International Law. The Popes of the middle ages determined many a hot dispute between rival forces without loss of human life. Their decrees were widely accepted. Their action however, at the best, could not adequately supply the place of a Rule of conduct to which all might indifferently appeal. And when, later, with the Reformation movement, the time came when the Pope could not command recognition as the Religious Head of a united Christendom, the necessity of the time quickened men's brains and, under the fostering care of the jurists of many lands, there began to emerge a system which gave shape and form to ideas generally received and largely acted on by nations.

What Sir James Stephen has eloquently said of religion may truly be predicated of International Law. The jurists set to music the tune which was haunting millions of ears. It was caught up, here and there, and repeated till the chorus was thundered out by a body of singers able to drown all discords and to force the vast unmusical mass to listen to them.

Although Hugo de Groot is regarded as the father and founder of International Law, he was preceded by two men born into the world forty years before him, namely, Ayala (the Spanish Judge-Advocate with the army of the Prince of Parma) and Suarez, (a Jesuit priest, also a Spaniard) both born in 1548, whose labors ought not to be forgotten.

Suarez in his "*De Legibus et Deo Legislatore*" and Ayala in his "*De Jure et Officiis Bellicis et Disciplina Militari*" had done good work.

Suarez, from the point of view of the Catholic theologian, assumes that the principles of the Moral Law are capable of complete and authoritative definition and are supported by the highest spiritual sanction. He therefore treats of the *Lex Naturalis* as a definite substantive law, sufficient and complete in its own sphere and binding on all men. But he regards International law as a code of rules dealing with matters outside the sphere of the Natural law:—matters not strictly right or wrong in themselves, but becoming so only by virtue of the precepts of the law which he considers to be founded upon the generally recognized usages of nations. In the following passage, which is interesting from the singular modernness of its spirit, he explains his view of the origin of International Law:

" The foundation of the law of Nations lies in this, that the human race, though divided into various peoples and kingdoms has always a certain unity, which is not merely the unity of species, but is also political and moral; as is shown by the natural precept of mutual love and pity, which extends to all peoples, however foreign they may be to one another, and whatever may be their character or constitution. From which it follows that although any state, whether a republic or a kingdom, may be a community complete in itself, it is nevertheless a member of that whole which constitutes the human race; for such a community is never so completely self-sufficing but that it requires some mutual help and intercourse with others, sometimes for the sake of some benefit to be obtained, but sometimes too, from the moral necessity and craving which are apparent from the very habits of mankind.

" On this account, therefore, a law is required by which states may be rightly directed and regulated in this kind of intercourse with one another. And although to a great extent this may be supplied by the Natural Law, still not adequately nor directly, and so it has come about that the usages of states have themselves led to the establishment of special rules. For, just as within an individual state custom gives rise to law, so for the human race as a whole, usages have led to the growth of the laws of nations; and this the more easily, inasmuch as the matters with which such law deals are few and are closely connected with the Law of Nature from which they may be deduced by inferences which, though not strictly necessary, so as to constitute laws of absolute moral obligation, still are very conformable and agreeable to nature, and therefore readily accepted by all."

Nor ought we to overlook the work of a writer even earlier than these. I mean Franciscus à victoria. Hall says of him that his writings in 1533 mark an era in the history of International Ethics. Spain claimed, largely by virtue of Papal grant and warrant, to acquire the territory and the mastery of the semi-civilized races of America. He denied the validity of the Papal Title; he maintained the sovereign rights of the aboriginal races, and he claimed to place international relations upon the basis of equal rights as between communities in actual possession of independence. In other words, he, first, clearly affirmed, the juridical principle of the complete international equality of independent states, however disproportionate their power.

Grotius undoubtedly had had the field of international relations explored by these, amongst other writers who had preceded him, but to him is certainly due the credit of evolving in his "*De Jure Belli ac Pacis*" a coherent system of law for the aggregation of states.

But I turn from this interesting line of thought, to consider, first, the part played by the United States in shaping the modern tendencies of International Law, and, next, whither those tendencies run. I have already spoken of the International writers of whom you are justly proud. It is not too much to say that the undoubted stream of tendency in modern International Law to mitigate the horrors of war, to humanize or to make less inhuman its methods, and to narrow the area of its consequential evils, is largely due to the policy of your Statesmen and the moral influence of your Jurists.

The reason why you thus early in your young history as an independent Power took so leading and noble a part in the domain of International Law is not far to seek;—it is at once obvious and interesting.

In the first place you were born late, in the life of the world, into the family of Nations. The common Law of England you had indeed imported and adopted as Colonists in some of the States, but subject as you then were to the Mother Country, you had no direct interest or voice in International relations, which were entirely within the domain of the Sovereign power. But when you asserted your Independence, the Laws of the Family of Nations, of which you then became a Member, were bound up with and became in part the justification for your existence as a sovereign power, and assumed for you importance and pre-eminence beyond the common law itself. Further, your remoteness from the conflicts of European powers and the wisdom of your Rulers in devoting their energies to the consolidation and development of home affairs gave to your people a special concern in that side of International Law which affects the interests, rights and obligations of Neutrals; and thus, it has come to pass that your writers have left their enduring mark on the Law of Nations touching allegiance, nationality, neutralization and neutrality, although as to these there are points which still remain indeterminate.

It is substantially true to say that while to earlier writers is mainly due the formulation of Rules relating to a state of War, to the United States,—to its judges, writers and statesmen, we largely owe the existing rules which relate to a state of peace and which affect the rights and obligations of powers, which, during a state of War, are themselves at Peace.

On the other hand, while in Great Britain, writers of great distinction on International Law are not wanting, and while the Judges of her Prize Courts have done a great work in systematizing and justifying on sound principles the Law of Capture and Prize, it is true to say that British Lawyers did not apply themselves, early, or with great zeal, to the consideration of International Jurisprudence.

Nor, again, is the reason far to seek. Great Britain had existed for centuries before International Law, in the modern sense, came into being. The main body of English Law was complete. The common law, springing from many sources, had assumed definite and comprehensive proportions. It sufficed for the needs of the time. Neither English Statesmen nor English Lawyers experienced the necessity which was strongly felt on the Continent of Europe — the constant theatre of War—for the formulation of rules of international conduct.

The need for these was slowly forced upon England, and, it is hardly too much to say that, to the British Admiral, accustomed to lord it on the High Seas, International Law at first came, not as a blessing and an aid, but, as a perplexing embarassment.

Notwithstanding all this, there is a marked agreement between English and American writers as to the manner in which International law is treated. They belong to the same school—a school distinctly different from that of writers on the Continent of Europe. The essential difference consists in this: Whereas in the latter, what I shall call the ethical and metaphysical treatment is followed, in the former, while not ignoring the important part, which Ethics play in the consideration of what International Law ought to be, its writers for the most part carefully distinguish between what is, in fact, International Law from their views of what the Law ought to be. Their treatment is mainly historical.

By most Continental writers, and by none more than Hautefeuille, what is, and what he thinks ought to be Law, theory and fact, Law and so-called rules of nature and of right, are mixed up in a way at once confusing and misleading.

One distinguished English writer indeed, the late Sir Henry Maine, thought that he had discovered a fundamental difference between English and American Jurists as to the view taken of the obligation of International Law.

His opinion was based on the Judgments of the English Judges in the celebrated *Franconia* case, in which it was held that the English Courts had no jurisdiction to try a foreigner for a crime committed on the High Seas although within a marine league from the British coast. The case was decided in 1876 and is reported in 2d Vol. of the Law Reports, Exchequer Division, p. 63. The facts were these: The Defendant was Captain Keyn, a German subject, in charge as Captain, of the German Steamship *Franconia*. When off Dover the *Franconia*, at a point within two and a half miles of the beach, ran into and sank a British steamer, *Strathclyde*, thereby causing loss of life. The facts were such as to constitute, according to English Law, the crime of manslaughter, of which the defendant was found guilty by the jury, but the learned Judge who tried the case at the Central Criminal Court reserved, for further consideration by the Court for Crown Cases Reserved, the question whether the Central Criminal Court had jurisdiction over the defendant, a foreigner, in respect of an offence committed by him on the High Seas, but within a marine league of the shore. All the members of the Court were of opinion that the chief Criminal Courts, that is to say, the Courts of Assize and the Central Criminal Court, were clothed with jurisdiction to administer justice in the bodies of counties, or, in other words, in English territory; and that from the time of Henry the VIII a court of special commissioners, and, later the Central Criminal Court (in which the defendant had been tried) had been invested by statute with the jurisdiction previously exercised by the Lord High Admiral on the High Seas. But the majority held that the marine league belt was not part of the territory of England, and therefore not within the bodies of counties, and also that the Admiral had had no jurisdiction over Foreigners on the High Seas. The minority, on the other hand, held that the marine belt was part of the territory of England and that the Admiral had had jurisdiction over Foreigners within those limits.

While I do not say that I should have arrived at the conclusions of historical fact of the majority, I am by no means clear that the judges of the United States, accepting the same data as did the majority of the English Judges, would not have decided in the same way. But however this may be, the views of the majority do not seem to me to warrant the assumption of Sir Henry Maine that the case fundamentally affects the view taken of the authority of International Law.

What it does incidentally reveal is a constitutional difference between the United States and Great Britain as to the methods by which the Municipal Courts acquire, at least in certain cases, jurisdiction to try and to punish offences against International Law.

An example of that difference is ready to hand. Improved and stricter views of neutral duties constitute one of the great developments of recent times.

These views were (for reasons to which I have already adverted) adopted earlier and more fully in the United States than in England. What was thereupon the action of the Executive? No sooner had Washington, as President, and Jefferson, as Secretary of State, promulgated the rules of neutrality by which they intended to be guided than they caused Gideon Henfield, an American citizen, to be tried for taking service on board a French Privateer, as being a criminal act, because in contravention of those Rules. Political feeling procured an acquittal, in spite of the Judge's direction.

Later no doubt Congress passed the Act of 1794, making such conduct criminal, not (as I gather,) because it was admitted to be necessary, but, simply to strengthen the hands of the Executive.

I can hardly doubt how the same case would have been dealt with in England.

Assuming the doing of the acts forbidden by Proclamation of neutrality, although infractions of International Law, not to be misdemeanors at common law, and not to have been made offences by Municipal Statute, the Judges (I cannot doubt) would have said the act was yesterday legal or at least not illegal and that, municipal law not having declared it a crime, they could not so declare it. According to the law of England a Proclamation by the Executive, in however solemn form, has no legislative force unless an Act of Parliament has so enacted. Parliament has in fact so enacted as to Orders of the Queen in Council in many cases. But assuming the law to be as I have stated, it points to no failure in England to recognize the full obligation of International Law as between States. For, notwithstanding isolated expressions of opinion uttered in times of excitement, it will not to-day be doubted that it is the duty of States to give effect to the obligations of International Law by Municipal legislation, where that is necessary, and, to use reasonable efforts to secure the observance of that law.

In England we have an old Constitution under which we are accustomed to fixed modes of Legislation, and when at last we accept a new development of International Law, we look to those methods to give effect to it. Indeed, that habit of looking to Legislation to meet new needs and developments, even in internal concerns, a habit confirmed and strengthened in the current century, has done much to restrain the Judges from that bold expansion of principle to meet new cases, which, when Legislation was less active, marked judicial utterances.

On the other hand, with you things are materially different. Your constitution is still so modern that equally fixed habits of looking to Legislation have not had time to grow up. Meanwhile that modern Constitution, is, from time to time, assailed by still more modern necessities, and the methods for its amendment are not swift or easy. The structure has not become completely ossified. Hence has arisen what I may call a flexibility of interpretation, applied to the constitution of the United States, for which I know no parallel in English judicature, and which seems to me to exceed the latitude of interpretation observed by your Judges in relation to Acts of Congress. I refer, as examples, to the emancipatian of the Slaves by President Lincoln during the Civil War, which was justified as an act covered by the necessities of the case and within the "war power" conferred on the Executive by the Constitution; and, also, to the judicial declaration, by the Supreme Court, of the validity of the Act of Congress making Greenbacks legal tender, on the ground that certain express powers, as to currency, being vested in Congress by the Constitution, the power of giving forced circulation to paper flowed from them as a desirable, if not a necessary, implication. With us no such difficulties arise. Our Constitution is unwritten, and, the Legislature is omnipotent. With you, the Constitution is written, and, the judicial power interprets it, and may declare the highest act of Congress null and void as unconstitutional. With us there can, in the strict sense of the words, be no such thing as an unconstitutional act of Parliament.

I turn now, to the consideration of what characterizes the later tendencies of International Law. In a word it is their greater humanity.

When Menelik, Emperor of Abyssinia, was recently reported to have cut off the right arms and feet of 500 prisoners, the civilized world felt a thrill of horror. Yet the time was when to treat prisoners as slaves and permanently to disable them from again bearing arms, were regarded as common incidents of belligerent capture. Such acts would once have excited no more indignation than did the inhumanities of the African Slave Trade before the days of Clarkson and Wilberforce.

Let us hope that it is no longer possible to do as Louis XIV did in his devastation of the Palatinate, or to do as he threatened to do, break down the dykes and overwhelm with disaster the Low countries. Let us hope, too, that no modern Napoleon would dare to decree as the first Napoleon did in his famous or infamous *seront brulées* edicts of 1810. The force of public opinion is too strong and it has reached a higher moral plane.

A bare recital of some of the important respects in which the evils of war have been mitigated by more humane customs must suffice.

Amongst them are: (1) the greater immunity from attack of the persons and property of enemy-subjects in a hostile country; (2) the restrictions imposed on the active operations of a Belligerent when occupying an enemy's country; (3) the recognised distinction between subjects of the enemy, combatant and non-combatant; (4) the deference accorded to Cartels, safe conducts and Flag of Truce; (5) the protection secured for ambulances and Hospitals and for all engaged in tending the sick and wounded—of which the Geneva Red Cross Convention of 1864 is a notable illustration; (6) the condemnation of the use of instruments of warfare which cause needless suffering.

In this field of humane work the United States took a prominent part. When the Civil War broke out President Lincoln was prompt in entrusting to Professor Franz Lieber the duty of preparing a Manual of systematized Rules for the conduct of forces in the Field—Rules aimed at the prevention of those scenes of cruelty and rapine which were formerly a disgrace to humanity. That Manual has, I believe, been utilized by the Governments of England, France and Germany.

Even more important are the changes wrought in the position of Neutrals in war times; who, while bound by strict obligations of neutrality, are in great measure left free and unrestricted in the pursuit of peaceful trade.

But in spite of all this who can say that these times breathe the spirit of Peace? There is War in the air. Nations armed to the teeth prate of Peace, but there is no sense of Peace. One sovereign burthens the industry of his people to maintain military and naval armament at war strength, and his neighbour does the like and justifies it by the example of the other; and Great Britain, insular though she be, with her Imperial Interests scattered the world over, follows, or is forced to follow, in the wake. If there be no War, there is at best an armed Peace.

Figures are appalling. I take those for 1895. In Austria the annual cost of Army and Navy was, in round figures, 18 millions sterling; in France 37 millions; in Germany 27 millions; in Great Britain 36 millions; in Italy 13 millions and in Russia 52 millions.

The significance of these figures is increased if we compare them with those of former times. The normal cost of the armaments of war has of late years enormously increased. The annual interest on the public debt of the Great Powers is a war tax. Behind this array of facts stands a tragic figure. It tells a dismal tale. It speaks of over-burthened industries, of a waste of human energy unprofitably engaged, of the squandering of treasure which might have let light into many lives, of homes made desolate, and all this, too often, without recompense in the thought that these sacrifices have been made for the love of country or to preserve national honour or for national safety. When will Governments learn the lesson that wisdom and justice in Policy are a stronger security than weight of armament?

> "Ah! when shall all men's good
> Be each man's Rule, and Universal Peace
> Lie, like a shaft of light, across the Land."

It is no wonder that men—earnest men—enthusiasts if you like, impressed with the evils of war, have dreamt the dream that the Millennium of Peace might be reached by establishing a universal system of International Arbitration.

The cry for Peace is an old world cry. It has echoed through all the ages, and arbitration has long been regarded as the handmaiden of Peace. Arbitration has, indeed, a venerable history of its own. According to Thucydides, the Historian of the Peloponnesian War, Archidamus, King of Sparta, declared that "it was unlawful to attack an enemy who offered to answer for his acts before a Tribunal of Arbiters."

The 50 years Treaty of Alliance between Argos and Lacedaemon contained a clause to the effect that if any difference should arise between the contracting parties, they should have recourse to the arbitration of a neutral Power, in accordance with the custom of their Ancestors. These views of enlightened Paganism have been re-inforced in Christian times. The Roman Emperors for a time, and afterwards in fuller measure the Popes (as we have seen) by their arbitrament often preserved the Peace of the old world and prevented the sacrifice of blood and treasure. But from time to time, and more fiercely when the influence of the Head of Christendom lessened, the passions of men broke out, the lust for Dominion asserted itself and many parts of Europe became so many fields of Golgotha. In our own times the desire has spread and grown strong for peaceful methods for the settlement of International disputes. The reason lies on the surface. Men and Nations are more enlightened; the grievous burthen of military armaments is sorely felt, and in these days when, broadly speaking, the people are enthroned, their views find free and forcible expression in a world-wide Press. The movement has been taken up by societies of thoughtful and learned men in many places. The *"Bureau International de la Paix"* records the fact that some 94 voluntary Peace Associations exist, of which some 40 are in Europe and 54 in America. Several Congresses have been held in Europe to enforce the same object, and in 1873 there was established at Ghent the *"Institut du Droit International,"* the declared objects of which are to put International Law on a scientific footing, to discuss and clear up moot points, and to substitute a system of rules conformable to right for the blind chances of force and the lavish expenditure of human life.

In 1873 also the Association for the Reform and Codification of the Law of Nations was formed, and it is to-day pursuing active Propaganda under the name of the International Law Association, which it adopted in 1894. It also has published a Report affirming the need of a system of International Arbitration.

In 1888 a Congress of Spanish and American Jurists was held at Lisbon, at which it was resolved that it was indispensable that a Tribunal of Arbitration should be constited with a view to avoid the necessity of war between nations.

But more hopeful still—the movement has spread to Legislative representative bodies. As far back as 1833 the Senate of Massachusetts proclaimed the necessity for some peaceful means of reconciling International differences, and affirmed the expediency of establishing a Court of Nations.

In 1890 the Senate and the House of Representatives of the United States adopted a concurrent Resolution, requesting the President to make use of any fit occasion to enter into negotiations with other Governments, to the end that any difference or dispute, which could not be adjusted by diplomatic agency, might be referred to arbitration and peacefully adjusted by such means.

The British House of Commons in 1893 responded by passing unanimously a Resolution expressive of the satisfaction it felt with the action of Congress, and of the hope that the Government of the Queen would lend its ready co-operation to give effect to it. President Cleveland officially communicated this last Resolution to Congress, and expressed his gratification that the sentiments of two great and kindred nations were thus authoritatively manifested in favour of the national and peaceable settlement of International quarrels by recourse to honourable arbitration. The Parliaments of Denmark, Norway, and Switzerland and the French Chamber of Deputies have followed suit.

It seemed eminently desirable that there should be some agency, by which members of the great Representative and Legislative Bodies of the World, interested in this far-reaching question, should meet on a common ground and discuss the basis for common action.

With this object there has recently been founded " The Permanent Parliamentary Committee in favour of Arbitration and Peace," or, as it is sometimes called " The Inter-Parliamentary Union." This Union has a permanent organisation—its office is at Berne. Its members are not vain Idealists. They are men of the world. They do not claim to be regenerators of mankind, nor do they promise the millennium, but they are doing honest and useful work in making straighter and less difficult, the path of intelligent progress. Their first formal meeting was held in Paris in 1889 under the Presidency of the late M. Jules Simon; their second in 1890 in London under the Presidency of Lord Herschell, ex-Lord Chancellor of Great Britain; their third in 1891 at Rome under the Presidency of Signor Bianchieri; their fourth in 1892 at Berne under the Presidency of M. Droz; their fifth in 1894 at the Hague under the Presidency of M. Rohnsen; their sixth in 1895 at Brussels under the Presidency of M. Deschamps; and their seventh will, it is arranged, be held this year at Buda-Pesth. Speaking in this place I need only refer, in passing, to the remarkable Pan-American Congress held in your States in 1890 at the instance of the late Mr. Blaine, directed to the same peaceful object.

It is obvious, therefore, that the sentiment for peace and in favour of Arbitration as the alternative for war, is growing apace. How has that sentiment told on the direct action of Nations? How far have they shaped their Policy according to its methods? The answers to these questions are also hopeful and encouraging.

Experience has shown that, over a large area, International differences may honourably, practically and usefully be dealt with by peaceful arbitrament. There have been since 1815 some sixty instances of effective International Arbitration. To thirty-two of these the United States have been a party and great Britain to some twenty of them.

There are many instances also of the introduction of Arbitration clauses into Treaties. Here again the United States appear in the van. Amongst the first of such Treaties—if not the very first—is the Guadaloupe-Hidalgo Treaty of 1848 between the United States and Mexico. Since that date many other countries have followed this example. In the year 1873 Signor Mancini recommended that, in all Treaties to which Italy was a party, such a clause should be introduced. Since the Treaty of Washington such clauses have been constantly inserted in Commercial, Postal and Consular Conventions. They are to be found also in the delimitation Treaties of Portugal with Great Britain and with the Congo Free State made in 1891. In 1895 the Belgian Senate, in a single day, approved of four Treaties with similar clauses, namely, Treaties concluded with Denmark, Greece, Norway and Sweden.

There remains to be mentioned a class of Treaties in which the principle of arbitration has obtained a still wider acceptance. The Treaties of 1888 between Switzerland and San Salvador, of 1888 between Switzerland and Ecuador, of 1888 between Switzerland and the French Republic and of 1894 between Spain and Honduras, respectively contain an agreement to refer all questions in difference, without exception, to arbitration. Belgium has similar Treaties with Venezuela, with the Orange Free State and with Hawaii.

These facts, dull as is the recital of them, are full of interest and hope for the future.

But are we thence to conclude that the Millennium of Peace has arrived—that the Dove bearing the olive branch has returned to the Ark, sure sign that the waters of international strife have permanently subsided?

I am not sanguine enough to lay this flattering unction to my soul. Unbridled ambition—thirst for wide dominion—pride of power still hold sway, although I believe with lessened force and in some sort under the restraint of the healthier opinion of the world.

But further, friend as I am of Peace, I would yet affirm that there may be even greater calamities than war—the dishonour of a nation, the triumph of an unrighteous cause, the perpetuation of hopeless and debasing tyranny:

> "War is honourable,
> In those who do their native rights maintain;
> In those whose swords an iron barrier are
> Between the lawless spoiler and the weak;
> But is, in those who draw th' offensive blade
> For added power or gain, sordid and despicable."

It behoves then all who are friends of Peace and advocates of Arbitration to recognise the difficulties of the question, to examine and meet these difficulties and to discriminate between the cases in which friendly Arbitration is, and in which it may not be, practically, possible.

Pursuing this line of thought, the short-comings of International Law reveal themselves to us and demonstrate the grave difficulties of the position.

The analogy between Arbitration as to matters in difference between individuals, and to matters in difference between nations, carries us but a short way.

In private litigation the agreement to refer is either enforceable as a rule of Court, or, where this is not so, the award gives to the successful litigant a substantive cause of action. In either case there is behind the Arbitrator the power of the Judge to decree, and the power of the Executive to compel compliance with, the behest of the Arbitrator. There exist elaborate rules of Court and provisions of the Legislature governing the practice of arbitrations. In fine, such arbitration is a mode of litigation by consent, governed by Law, starting from familiar rules, and carrying the full sanction of Judicial decision. International Arbitration has none of these characteristics. It is a cardinal principle of the Law of Nations that each sovereign power, however politically weak, is internationally equal to any other power, however politically strong. There are no Rules of International Law relating to arbitration, and of the Law itself there is no authoritative exponent nor any recognized authority for its enforcement.

But there are differences to which, even as between individuals, arbitration is inapplicable—subjects which find their counterpart in the affairs of nations. Men do not arbitrate where character is at stake, nor, will any self-respecting nation readily arbitrate on questions touching its national independence or affecting its honour.

Again, a nation may agree to arbitrate and then repudiate its agreement. Who is to coerce it? Or, having gone to arbitration and been worsted it may decline to be bound by the Award. Who is to compel it?

These considerations seem to me to justify two conclusions:— The first is that arbitration will not cover the whole field of International controversy, and the second that unless and until the Great Powers of the World, in League, bind themselves to coerce a recalcitrant member of the Family of Nations—we have still to face the more than possible disregard by powerful States of the obligations of good faith and of justice. The scheme of such a combination has been advocated, but the signs of its accomplishment are absent. We have, as yet, no League of Nations of the Amphictyonic type.

Are we then to conclude that Force is still the only power that rules the world? Must we then say that the sphere of arbitration is a narrow and contracted one?

By no means. The sanctions which restrain the wrongdoer—the breaker of public faith—the disturber of the peace of the world, are not weak, and, year by year, they wax stronger. They are the dread of war and the reprobation of mankind. Public opinion is a force which makes itself felt in every corner and cranny of the world, and is most powerful in the communities most civilized. In the public Press and in the Telegraph, it possesses agents by which its power is concentrated, and speedily brought to bear where there is any public wrong to be exposed and reprobated. It year by year gathers strength as general enlightenment extends its empire, and a higher moral altitude is attained by mankind. It has no ships of war upon the seas or armies in the field, and yet great Potentates tremble before it and humbly bow to its Rule.

Again Trade and Travel are great pacificators. The more Nations know of one another, the more Trade relations are established between them, the more goodwill and mutual interest grow up; and, these are powerful agents working for Peace.

But although I have indicated certain classes of questions on which sovereign powers may be unwilling to arbitrate, I am glad to think that these are not the questions which most commonly lead to war. It is hardly too much to say that Arbitration may fitly be applied in the case of by far the largest number of questions which lead to International differences. Broadly stated, (1) wherever the right in dispute will be determined by the ascertainment of the true facts of the case; (2) where, the facts being ascertained, the right depends on the application of the proper principles of International Law to the given facts and (3) where the dispute is one which may properly be adjusted on a give-and-take principle, with due provision for equitable compensation, as in cases of delimitation of territory and the like—in such cases, the matter is one which ought to be arbitrated.

The question next arises what ought to be the constitution of the Tribunal of Arbitration? Is it to be a Tribunal *ad hoc*, or is it to be a permanent International Tribunal?

It may be enough to say, that at this stage, the question of the constitution of a permanent Tribunal is not ripe for practical discussion, nor will it be until the majority of the Great Powers have given in their adhesion to the principle. But whatever may be said for vesting the authority in such Powers to select the Arbitrators, from time to time, as occasion may arise, I doubt whether in any case a permanent Tribunal, the members of which shall be *a priori* designated, is practicable or desirable. In the first place what, in the particular case, is the best Tribunal must largely depend upon the question to be arbitrated. But apart from this, I gravely doubt the wisdom of giving that character of permanence to the *personnel* of any such Tribunal. The interests involved are commonly so enormous and the forces of national sympathy, pride and prejudice, are so searching, so great and so subtle, that I doubt whether a Tribunal, the membership of which had a character of permanence, even if solely composed of men accustomed to exercise the judicial faculty, would long retain general confidence, and, I fear, it might gradually assume intolerable pretensions.

There is danger, too, to be guarded against from another quarter. So long as War remains the sole Court wherein to try International quarrels, the risks of failure are so tremendous, and, the mere rumour of war so paralyses commercial and industrial life, that pretensions wholly unfounded will rarely be advanced by any nation, and, the strenuous efforts of statesmen, whether immediately concerned or not, will be directed to prevent war. But if there be a standing Court of Nations, to which any power may resort, with little cost and no risk, the temptation may be strong to put forward pretentious and unfounded claims, in support of which there may readily be found, in most countries, (can we except even Great Britain and the United States?) busybody Jingoes only too ready to air their spurious and inflammatory patriotism.

There is one influence which by the Law of Nations may be legitimately exercised by the Powers in the interests of Peace— I mean Mediation.

The Plenipotentiaries assembled at the Congress of Paris, 1856, recorded the following admirable sentiments in their 23rd protocol: "The Plenipotentiaries do not hesitate to express, in the names of their Governments, the wish that States between which any serious misunderstanding may arise should, before appealing to arms, have recourse as far as circumstances may allow to the good offices of a friendly power. The Plenipothentiaries hope that the Governments not represented at the Congress will unite in the sentiment which has inspired the wish recorded in the present protocol."

In the treaty which they concluded they embodied, but with a more limited application, the principle of mediation, more formal than that of good offices, though substantially similar to it. In case of a misunderstanding between the Porte and any of the signatory powers, the obligation was undertaken "before having recourse to the use of force, to afford the other contracting parties the opportunity of preventing such an extremity by means of their mediation." (Art. 8). Under this article Turkey, in 1877, appealed to the other powers to mediate between her and Russia. It is not, perhaps, to be wondered at, considering the circumstances, that the appeal did not succeed in preventing the Russo-Turkish War. But the powers assembled in the African Conference at Berlin were not discouraged from repeating the praiseworthy attempt, and in the final act of that Conference the following proviso (Article 12) appears:—

"In case of a serious disagreement arising between the signatory powers on any subjects within the limits of the Territory mentioned in Article 1 and placed under the *regime* of commercial freedom, the Powers mutually agree, before appealing to arms, to have recourse to the mediation of one or more of the neutral powers."

It is to be noted that this provision contemplates not arbitration but mediation, which is a different thing. The Mediator is not, at least, in the first instance, invested, and does not seek to be invested, with authority to adjudicate upon the matter in difference. He is the friend of both parties. He seeks to bring them together. He avoids a tone of dictation to either. He is careful to avoid, as to each of them, anything which may wound their political dignity or their susceptibilities. If he cannot compose the quarrel, he may at least narrow its area and probably roduce it to more limited dimensions, the result of mutual concessions; and, having narrowed the issues, he may pave the way for a final settlement by a reference to arbitration or by some other method.

This is a Power often used, perhaps not so often as it ought to be—and with good results.

It is obvious that it requires tact and judgment, as to mode, time and circumstance, and that the task can be undertaken hopefully, only where the Mediator possesses great moral influence, and, where he is beyond the suspicion of any motive except desire for Peace and the public good.

There is, perhaps, no class of question in which mediation may not, time and occasion being wisely chosen, be usefully employed, even in delicate questions affecting national honour and sentiment.

Mr. President, I come to an end. I have but touched the fringe of a great subject. No one can doubt that sound and well-defined rules of International Law conduce to the progress of civilization and help to ensure the Peace of the World.

In dealing with the subject of arbitration I have thought it right to sound a note of caution, but it would, indeed, be a reproach to our nineteen centuries of Christian civilization, if there were now no better method, for settling international differences, than the cruel and debasing methods of war. May we not hope that the people of these States and the people of the Mother Land—kindred peoples—may, in this matter, set an example, of lasting influence, to the world? They are blood relations. They are indeed separate and independent peoples but neither regards the other as a Foreign nation.

We boast of our advance and often look back with pitying contempt on the ways and manners of generations gone by. Are we ourselves without reproach? Has our Civilization borne the true marks? Must it not be said, as has been said of Religion itself, that countless crimes have been committed in its name? Probably it was inevitable that the weaker races should, in the end, succumb, but have we always treated them with consideration and with justice? Has not civilization too often been presented to them at the point of the bayonet and the Bible by the hand of the Filibuster? And apart from races we deem barbarous, is not the passion for dominion and wealth and power accountable for the worst chapters of cruelty and oppression written in the World's History? Few peoples —perhaps none—are free from this reproach. What indeed is true Civilization? By its fruit you shall know it. It is not dominion, wealth, material luxury; nay, not even a great Literature and Education wide spread—good though these things be. Civilization is not a veneer; it must penetrate to the very heart and core of societies of men.

Its true signs are thought for the poor and suffering, chivalrous regard and respect for woman, the frank recognition of human brotherhood, irrespective of race or colour or nation or religion, the narrowing of the domain of mere force as a governing factor in the world, the love of ordered freedom, abhorrence of what is mean and cruel and vile, ceaseless devotion to the claims of justice. Civilization in that, its true, its highest sense, must make for Peace. We have solid grounds for faith in the Future. Government is becoming more and more, but in no narrow class sense, government of the people by the people and for the people. Populations are no longer moved and manoeuvred as the arbitrary will or restless ambition or caprice of Kings or Potentates may dictate. And although democracy is subject to violent gusts of passion and prejudice, they are gusts only. The abiding sentiment of the masses is for peace—for peace to live industrious lives and to be at rest with all mankind. With the Prophet of old they feel—though the feeling may find no articulate utterance—"how beautiful upon the mountains are the feet of him that bringeth good tidings, that publisheth peace."

Mr. President, I began by speaking of the two great divisions—American and British—of that English speaking world which you and I represent to-day, and with one more reference to them I end.

Who can doubt the influence they possess for ensuring the healthy progress and the peace of mankind? But if this influence is to be fully felt, they must work together in cordial friendship, each people in its own sphere of action. If they have great power, they have also great responsibility. No cause they espouse can fail; no cause they oppose can triumph. The future is, in large part, theirs. They have the making of history in the times that are to come. The greatest calamity that could befall would be strife which should divide them.

Let us pray that this shall never be. Let us pray that they, always self-respecting, each in honour upholding its own Flag, safeguarding its own Heritage of right and respecting the rights of others, each in its own way fulfilling its high national destiny, shall yet work in harmony for the Progress and the Peace of the World.